JAY LONG

refined.

300 SOUTH MEDIA GROUP

◈

NEW YORK

This book is presented as a collection.

ISBN-13: 978-1-957596-06-8

First Printing August 2022
Book & Cover Design: Indie Author Solutions
Published by 300 South Media Group

To the four who influenced me most: my Mom, Dad, Pop-Pop, and Aunt Mare. Each have taught me in their own way, that there are endless possibilities in life, but time is limited.

Preface ═══════

Many years ago, I started writing screenplays, because it was what I had hoped to do. At the time, resources weren't as they are today, and I never made the leap to the West Coast, which is where one had to go to break in as a screenwriter. In my 2nd-year college English class my professor introduced me to the writings of Robert Frost. I knew then I wanted to change the world with my words. I have aspired to be part of a writing community for decades. In November of 2015, my first poetry collection, Timeless Chatter Between the Heart and Mind, was published, and I've never looked back. Thank you, Robert Frost, for the 'Road Not Taken'...you have made all the difference.

Honestly, it's what pushes me through the most trying of times. All of my life, I have taken the path I felt was best for me, and more times than not, it's been the one less traveled.

═══════ ◈ ═══════

refined.

In life, if we're lucky, we'll always have someone who adds to our shine by sharing theirs. Those connections are our personal lighthouses. They're a beacon of hope, stability, and understanding through storms and fair weather. The beauty of receiving unconditional light is it passes through us all so we can be that for another. Our reflections reach far greater than we can ever imagine. We touch countless lives without ever realizing it. You never know when you will be the only light burning in someone's darkness. Keep shining, so they can find you.

＝＝＝＝＝ ◈ ＝＝＝＝＝

Soul mates. Twin flames. They aren't always lovers. There are those we connect with on a much deeper level than love could ever encompass. Those are our people. Those are our soul mates. They're the ones we've never had to question where they stood with us, how we fit into their lives. But even more so, we don't remember what life was like without them because it feels as if they've always been there.

＝＝＝＝＝ ◈ ＝＝＝＝＝

═══════════ ◆ ═══════════

Pride has taken more than its fair share of relationships. Not just relationships with others but with ourselves. How often do we not go somewhere, call someone, or do what makes us happy because of something so minor? I'm sure it didn't feel little at the time, but in the big picture of life, it honestly is. There's a reason why pride is one of the seven deadly sins because it causes internal grief. The damage we do to ourselves will always cut the deepest and leave the most significant scars.

═══════════ ◆ ═══════════

―――――― ◈ ――――――

When we finally realize what our calling in life is, there's no stopping until we are on that path. Nothing else matters—the struggles before were preparing you for what's to come. Consider it a baptism by fire, and you are its forged steel.

―――――― ◈ ――――――

━━━━━━━ ◆ ━━━━━━━

From time to time, we all have put our dreams aside for one reason or another. Those who step out of their comfort zone to chase a dream or find their passion and fully embrace it are those who are genuinely at peace. Failure is not the cause of a soul's death... it's regret.

━━━━━━━ ◆ ━━━━━━━

Everything we experience holds a price. In its purest form, the cost of living is dying and inevitable for all of us.

It's been said this notion is morbid, but it's the most factual statement I have ever made. Every single human will one day return to the Earth. There is no escaping that fate. What we do with our limited time is our choice. How others remember us is our legacy.

I have done my best never to take the road of less resistance. Sometimes by choice but mainly because situations arose causing the high road—the one with the most obstacles and hurdles to be the lane I needed to maneuver. "Navigation" has become second nature to me; like breathing, it simply happens. It has made a difference. There have been times when I've raised my hands in anguish and prayed for an easy ride. Then I remind myself there's no easy button in life. I know that, though my results are sometimes delayed, the outcome is always better at the end of the day. I'm grateful for my blessings and understanding of my blocks.

═══════ ◆ ═══════

Time is one thing we cannot control. It can't be stopped, rewound, fast-forwarded, or experienced again. Tomorrow is never promised, so be sure to spend it the best you can every day you can.

═══════ ◆ ═══════

———— ◆ ————

Sometimes overnight success can take 20 years. You never know when you're one story, idea, review, client, or day away from making all of your dreams come true. Set small goals and celebrate each victory.

———— ◆ ————

Far too many are willing to sacrifice true happiness not to be lonely, to fill in their time, or to try and make things work that possibly aren't ideal for their own situation. We all want love, but that doesn't mean it needs to be rushed into with the pressure for it to be "the one." Relationships are hard enough without that be-all, end-all expectations. Enjoy whatever love comes your way. It will evolve as it should.

═══════ ◆ ═══════

Complacency is detrimental to peace. Eventually, all we allow or ignore will come back around if we don't handle it. We need to do our best to be proactive in life rather than reactive.

═══════ ◆ ═══════

———— ◈ ————

Laugh every chance you can. Life is far too short to spend it any other way than happy. Find it within yourself and never depend on someone else to provide that happiness—it's not there. Look no further than yourself.

———— ◈ ————

Although we will never know if the choices we make between two or more things are the right ones or how it would turn out if we chose differently, we are granted certain aspects of positivity or negativity in ways of seeing how things pan out. The important thing is never to doubt yourself. You've made the decision. Stick with it because the 'what if?' can never be answered.

===== ◈ =====

Loss on any level can feel like a piece of you is gone. The heart is always the last to leave the fight. It's the last to lose hope, and it's the last to heal. Know your heart will "beat" again. Healing is personal. Whenever a loss occurs, allow yourself to mourn without boundaries or set times.

===== ◈ =====

———————— ◆ ————————

The heart wants what it wants. That also holds true for what it doesn't want. We all have wants, wishes, and desires, but each comes with natural boundaries. No one should be mistreated because they know what doesn't feel right or work for them.

———————— ◆ ————————

———— ◆ ————

Beautiful sometimes isn't enough. There are those we meet in our lives that words cannot describe. Don't try. They're golden moments of light within your life. Just cherish them; they're few and far between.

———— ◆ ————

=========== ◆ ===========

I feel if you wait for perfection and change your life to do so, you're not living life; you're allowing life to carry you. Live your best life, even if that means you make mistakes. Perfection is a lie far too many believe. The smiles of those you love hold the only true perfection. Absolute perfection comes when happiness is your number one goal.

Do you want perfect? Wake up happy every day.

=========== ◆ ===========

Each day brings a brand-new dawn. But it cannot erase the choices made yesterday. It cannot mend the wounds of lost hope or heal the scars of the past. The rising sun is not a free pass to simply 'wait and see' what's to come. A new day offers an opportunity, a moment in time to capture the magic of tomorrow by making the most of today.

———————— ◆ ————————

We share our days with so many good-hearted people. Often, those relationships we build become our best friends, not lovers, but the experience is sometimes more significant. For those souls, we flame on with, be sure to cherish them. Love them and never let them forget what they mean to you.

———————— ◆ ————————

—— ◈ ——

The little things in life are indeed what matters. It's not the extravagant gifts. It's the moments—those mini escapes from all that surrounds us. It's the gesture that comes with the little things. It's the smiles that we share with the little things. It's the laughter we create from the little things. Never underestimate each of those moments in our life; it's where the memories are made.

—— ◈ ——

———— ◆ ————

Throughout our lives, we experience things causing us to build walls. So often, we find others who have suffered or experienced the same or more. It's hard to break down the barriers created when they are meant to protect your heart but always try. If you have built the wall, try to be open to letting some of it crumble because magic also enters through closed doors.

———— ◆ ————

During your proudest moments, those days of undeniable strength when each step you take rises you above it all, keep an open heart and remember, in your darkest hours, those nights you feel your weakest when every breath leaves you broken, love will always find a way.

========= ◆ =========

We truly live two lives. The one where we are physically here walking this Earth. And the 2nd is when we become memories of those we left behind. We are truly never gone until the last memory of us is forgotten. It's essential to make sure that we do all we can to make the memories of us the best they can be for all of those around us.

========= ◆ =========

=========== ◆ ===========

We need to be true to ourselves because, at the end of the day, we're responsible for the path we travel. Take control of your days. Allow yourself to be happy and say no to people and things that do not add to that happiness.

=========== ◆ ===========

———— ◆ ————

Experience is a great influencer. It provides incredible insight. It serves as an internal set of eyes to see all that goes unnoticed. Our learned history equips us with a beautiful light to navigate even the darkest days, find the safest path through each day, and helps us find shelter to wait out the fiercest storms.

———— ◆ ————

―――――― ◆ ――――――

Sometimes each of us in our life, unfortunately, finds the wrong love during our searching. It takes a lot to open up and love again, but when you find the one who compliments you, it's almost as if the world stops spinning for a while. You can also put your guard down and knock a little bit of those walls to the side. The heart doesn't need a cage to beat in; it needs another heart to hold.

―――――― ◆ ――――――

---◆---

What happens when the truths become lies? It certainly makes it challenging to know what to believe. Lies are temporary fixes for an underlying issue. Once the pieces start to fall away, there is no denying what has deceitfully been buried. Most untruths are set into place to benefit the ones offering them. The true tragedy of life comes from those who manipulate, swindle, and use others' empathy and compassion as the opportunity to benefit themselves. Time usually exposes what's been meant to be hidden. A scramble typically follows—a mad dash to explain away the obvious. As if that will somehow make the wrong right. All it does is kill trust. Once that's lost, there is never another "the way it used to be."

---◆---

Memories can be wonderful, except when they're not. We all have them: snapshots that fill our minds with hurt, fear, pain, or anguish. It frames a time in our lives because of its negative impact. During those days, it's essential to do our best not to relive those moments. All we can do is push through the best we can, knowing we survived.

========= ◈ =========

When all else fails, take in all the beauty that surrounds you. Cherish each breath and seize every day as if it's your last, for everything is possible with a heart that is full.

========= ◈ =========

I think we all have the one person in our lives who encompasses everything we've ever experienced. It's as if they are otherworldly, sent here to compliment and complete our world. They are that uncontrollable force.

———— ◆ ————

If each day is met with contempt, your travels will all be uphill. Celebrate the day upon its own merit until no more battles are left to win. Find the riches in each breath granted and fight, not with the sword, but with the will to see a better tomorrow. And although the setting sun is not a sign of salvation, it is a reminder of another day passing where you endured all life had for you, both good and bad.

———— ◆ ————

———— ◈ ————

The trials of our daily lives can seem unfair and, at times, unrelenting. Just remember everything is temporary, even pain and the hurt associated with loss. Allow yourself to bend, but never fully shatter.

———— ◈ ————

═══════════ ◆ ═══════════

Life meets all of us with a full fist at times. We all seem to lose a piece of ourselves along the way. For many, there's a distinct line between youth and everything that happens after. It's real. It's redeemable. But don't allow it to cash in on dreams—they're what keeps us young.

═══════════ ◆ ═══════════

Never fear the darkness. It's only because of it that we can appreciate the light. We find our strength, our drive, not by leaning on others, but from within. Challenging times are when we see our true selves, and our audacious nature of living life fully is born.

═══════ ◈ ═══════

Everything we want in life can be attained. Our wildest dreams have no boundaries; if you remain steady and stable, you can reach those goals. Far too many want the view from the mountain top but aren't willing to set out on the climb. I can guarantee the reward is worth it and the view is absolutely spectacular.

═══════ ◈ ═══════

Experience brings an empathetic purity that cannot be understood unless you've been there. We know what it means to be hurt. For that reason, hardened hearts beat much more freely. Doing so without expectations. Instead, facing each moment as they arise.

―――――― ◆ ――――――

At the end of the day, as long as those I hold dear to me are still with me, life is OK. If each morning I am given the grace to try and make a difference in the lives of others while doing what I love, life is OK. If I lay my head to rest each night, and the dreams I have are still intact, life is OK. So many need to conquer and be right when all we truly need to do is have empathy and to encourage. We have to keep everything in perspective. If the abovementioned things remain my truth, nothing else matters.

―――――― ◆ ――――――

═══════ ◆ ═══════

You can't flourish when your choices lead to diminishing oneself rather than growing. So many choose chaos over serenity and then wonder why their days are endless. There is no found freedom when locked in a prison of self-sabotage.

═══════ ◆ ═══════

——————— ◈ ———————

Our life isn't always pretty, but some moments are simply beautiful. Times of struggle are often filled with undeniable grace. And during those days of lost battles and bitter truths, the mercy of hope will find you and guide you along your way.

——————— ◈ ———————

We get so lost in the idea that everything must be perfect. Perfection is unreachable. Not because things can't be perfect, but we are never satisfied with how things are. Allow the flaws to show true beauty in every aspect of life. Yes, sunsets are beautiful, but we can't wish away the entire day in order to get to it; think of all we'd miss.

There's nothing more beautiful than watching the warrior finally find their way. Tattered, torn, weathered, and worn, yes, but whole. Withstanding life's trials takes all we have. Some days that's not very much, but when defeat is not an option, each moment is its own reward. For those who face the darkness, may you find strength each day until the light again surrounds you.

=========== ◆ ===========

Memories don't always have to be big-money gifts or huge once-in-a-lifetime trips. Memories are whatever it is that connects us. The moments we share with ourselves, or others become the bookmarks of our lives. I can only hope when they turn the final page of mine and the book closes, it's riddled with dog-eared pages of just how beautiful life truly is.

=========== ◆ ===========

———————— ◇ ————————

Love, empathy, and understanding will always win. They are what dreams soar on when the wind beneath them loses momentum. Choose kindness, and you'll never truly fail. Some want you to fall. Prove them wrong—so many wish to judge and conquer when goodwill and mercy are all that's genuinely needed.

———————— ◇ ————————

How wonderful this world could be if always looked at through the eyes of a child, ravenous for knowledge, forever ready for a new adventure. Each day would be filled with honesty and truth. Beauty would be seen most innocently and sincerely. Imagine how simple and carefree life would be without judgment and the understanding of loss.

---◆---

This is the edge of tomorrow. The moments separate what we know and all that awaits to be discovered. Love one another today because the world as we know it is changing before our eyes.

---◆---

━━━━━━━━ ◆ ━━━━━━━━

One of the most important days of my life was
when I forgave myself for not always doing what
was in my best interest. I allowed the past to be
just that—done. I could understand how the
days gone by all served as lessons, and I no
longer had control over them. What I did have
was a responsibility to ensure every day going
forward was lived with purpose the best I could
every day I could.

━━━━━━━━ ◆ ━━━━━━━━

Just like art, we are all unique and priceless. You are someone's every thought, their scribbled lines of rhyme. You are someone's 11:11 wish and every moment of their tomorrow. You are more than ink stains on a page. You are an unpublished masterpiece waiting to be found.

We live in a time that is much different than anything we've ever seen or come to know. Our nation has become separated. We, as a whole, need to find a balance between caring for ourselves and holding compassion for our fellow man and woman. The only way to do that is to remain steady and stable. To survive as one, each of us must be self-sufficient and reliable along the journey. Let acceptance and love shine bright to light the way. Our actions will be the fuel that feeds the fire for change.

———— ◆ ————

We are our own landscape—nature's beautiful canvas that time and experience work on to create a masterpiece. Our scratches and cracks are our blessings. As we grow and evolve, many days of affliction are looked back on with tormented eyes. Yes, they may be tough, even outright horrible, but know you survived. You survived each of them to find the being you are today. Life is more about beautiful flaws than its perfection. In time I hope your durability brings reassurance of just how much of a treasure you are.

———— ◆ ————

I look in the mirror and miss the innocence that once stared back at me. Where have our yesterdays gone? The golden days of youth sit tucked away in the corners of my mind as still frame memories. Why do we wish away the days and look to turn the pages of our story so quickly? The minutes should be measured by smiles and sorrow ticked away in seconds. If I could, I'd relive them all line by line. Then, each bookmark would hold an unmistakable place in time. Never fail to capture each day and savor the daily miracles - create your own masterpiece without the fear of missing a moment.

═══════ ◈ ═══════

Funny how things change. As we get older, many things we took for granted all hit differently. Even song lyrics we simply jammed to in our younger years hold a deeper meaning. Experience will do that to you. It creates understanding. It reveals truth. Life is about perspective; nothing teaches that more than the years we leave behind.

═══════ ◈ ═══════

═══════ ◈ ═══════

We seem to find ourselves 'caged' from time to time. Whether by our own doing or allowing others to take some of the wind from underneath our wings. It's important to recognize this as soon as possible. Progress, personal growth, and ultimately freedom aren't achieved by standing still or putting limits on who we are. We're born to run, to seek the highest peak, and reach our full potential. Life needs to be lived, not simply accepted.

═══════ ◈ ═══════

═══════ ◈ ═══════

It's natural to experience the loss of love or even go through a bad relationship, where the red flags weren't seen until things got going. Those types of relationships, at their core, prepare us for the beautiful ones. Remember, no matter what happened in the past, you're worthy of love and are enough.

═══════ ◈ ═══════

═══════ ◈ ═══════

We all possess an unimaginable amount of fight inside ourselves. And when the conflict within one's soul teams up with the determination in their mind and the hope in their heart, nothing can stop them.

═══════ ◈ ═══════

———— ◈ ————

Life has a mind of its own. It never plays fair. I've never considered myself lucky. There are moments when I've caught up to destiny because of hard work and perseverance. During the times I've been fortunate enough to stay in stride, life rewarded me.

———— ◈ ————

===== ◆ =====

There is no manual for navigating through life. There's a constant mix of joys, disappointments, laughter, love, and loss. The hardest of which is the gradual learning that comes after sudden change.

===== ◆ =====

═══════ ◆ ═══════

When life is continually lived chasing 'the why' there's a certain solace in finding a quiet corner to escape one's inner thoughts. Hurt takes its toll on the soul. Wisdom offers a deeper kind of pain. It no longer renders one devastated; it's more a profound feeling of disappointment. If each experience is absorbed and internalized, it will create a space within the heart and mind where darkness rules. Do not depend on others to illuminate your days. Become the shine. Allow the glow from within to light the way out of the shadows.

═══════ ◆ ═══════

No one can steal your truth. Remember that! What others perceive cannot take away from the meaning you hold within. Never miss the moments life puts in front of you. Those countless reminders as it unfolds. Grow from every negative and positive experience because the good will always outweigh the bad. Life's beauty is in the bloom, and the answers are often found in the waiting.

———— ◈ ————

Don't live with despair but remember there is nothing wrong with having a bit of a now or never attitude when it comes to living. Days seem to melt into each other; before you know it, another year has passed. Destinations, get-togethers, and celebrations all seem to find their way into hiding. In contrast, sixty-hour work weeks, bills, and worry grab the spotlight. Responsibilities, of course, must be met, but at what cost? Take time to find the balance between work and play. Enjoy the simple things in life. Tomorrow is never guaranteed. So stop making plans to make plans. Life is lived one day at a time. Make each one count.

———— ◈ ————

During nights you feel as if you're not brave, never live in fear. Hidden in all the darkness, you will find the light. Self-love and self-awareness will give you the courage to see that tomorrow is a brighter day.

===== ◈ =====

As with most good things in life, love doesn't need extravagant efforts. The little things do mean the most.

Show up and be present because showing actual effort is a game-changer for life.

===== ◈ =====

Without communication, there's no sense, really. How can we be a compliment to anyone or vice-versa if wants, needs, kinks, turn-ons, fears, wishes, and dreams can't be shared? Communication, trust, empathy, understanding, and patience are all must-have components of any loving relationship. Without them, there will always be an incomplete connection.

---◇---

I have never fallen and stayed there. I gathered my thoughts, dusted myself off, and rose back up. I'll never quit. I'll never give up. I stand before you proudly as one who has survived the fall and felt the cold Earth against his cheek. Like the pillars of a great metropolis, my legs have weakened, but my soul is not torn. No burden I bear shall ever hold me down, nor will the wars of my past ever leave me lifeless.

---◇---

There is nowhere to run from the wild ride of living. We are each met with uphill climbs, and at times, the hurdles along the way seem insurmountable. No more factual statement about life has been made than 'No One Gets Out Alive.' So go on the adventure. Take a nap. Don't be a bully. Eat the cookie. Have cereal for dinner. Stay in bed past noon on a Sunday. Meet friends for drinks. Kiss the girl or the boy or both. Buy the dress. Visit Paris. Love unconditionally. Tell the truth. Fight for those who cannot fight. Paint. Stand up for what you believe. Write. Sing in the shower and the car and at karaoke. And when you run out of things to do, do them all again. You'll be glad you did.

═══════════ ◈ ═══════════

Waking up to another day is a blessing that many take for granted. Those who have suffered loss understand that within a minute—a split second—the privilege can be taken away. Stay humble and squeeze every moment out of each day. Cherish the days. Our time is limited, and the sooner we realize that the freer we become.

═══════════ ◈ ═══════════

How often do we use fear as an excuse to:

—get to know someone

—start a relationship

—stay in a relationship

The list can go on and on. We limit ourselves because of fear and doubt. I think the critical thing to remember is fear will always be there, regardless, and doubt is just the product of that fear. So why stifle who you are because of it?

———————— ◆ ————————

Never take for granted the broken-hearted willing to love. They shine on even if the light is fractured. Inner beauty is never broken. The pieces may be shattered, but the vessel is pristine. The truth is, love always takes a part of you, and sometimes ties aren't ever severed clean. The scars will heal, but the heart seldom truly mends—it just learns to set itself ablaze since there's an insatiable need to find its lost beat.

———————— ◆ ————————

—— ◆ ——

True soul mates are a welcomed rarity. Look for that partner who compliments you, not completes you. You aren't missing pieces; you're whole and offering yourself 100%. The pressure of your happiness should not be placed on someone else. That comes from within. Happiness, although palpable, is not tangible—the 'switch' is within you.

—— ◆ ——

—————— ◆ ——————

Artists generally don't usually forget people who have touched their lives. Relationships, on all levels, bring inspiration and have accounted for so much excellent writing, great art, and beautiful music. The connections are immortalized through those creations.

—————— ◆ ——————

———— ◇ ————

So many silently sit back and accept the actions of others when it comes to a matter of the heart. Tolerance speaks much louder than words. Never beg to be loved. The heart must realize its worth.

———— ◇ ————

---◈---

I always take the week between Christmas and the New Year to reflect on the past year. I stopped with the whole "new year, new me" idea long ago. I simply try to do the best I can every day I can. I set short and long-term goals and keep my focus on them. I believe better days are ahead, and I'm looking forward to waking up to each of them.

---◈---

━━━━━ ◆ ━━━━━

I love when home becomes the person you cherish most. No matter where they roam, your home is intact and every step you take is on your way back.

━━━━━ ◆ ━━━━━

———— ◆ ————

We never see the struggles or the past heartaches leading to a person finding that perfect love. We are just witnesses to the end result. Each of us has backstories and lost loves. We all have mistakes that haunt us. With any luck, we find the person who accepts all of it.

———— ◆ ————

———— ◈ ————

We always seem to be rushing everything. From our day to our week, to our month, to our year— we turn the pages too quickly. We wish our time away to get to the next 'thing.' Remember, we have limited time, but the possibilities are endless. Slow down. Take a breath. Enjoy the surroundings, even if they're not ideal. Each experience teaches us some type of lesson.

———— ◈ ————

========= ◆ =========

It needs to be looked at differently if you can't currently get out of the Monday-Friday race. You're not living your best life by living for Friday and dreading Mondays. In fact, you might be wasting your time, and you may best serve yourself by doing a little soul searching for your true passion and doing your best to gravitate towards that.

========= ◆ =========

—— ◈ ——

No matter what we think of ourselves, we are perfect in someone else's eyes.

—— ◈ ——

―――――― ◆ ――――――

Long-distance relationships can work, but they take effort from both individuals. Trust is the most significant factor in keeping it all together. I won't say that long-distance relationships are better, but in today's day and age, I understand why they work.

By being apart more than those who may live with each other or in the same town, the time spent together is dedicated to only each other. Wouldn't it be wonderful if all those fortunate enough to spend each day with their love, partner, and significant other were as devoted?

―――――― ◆ ――――――

======= ◆ =======

Nothing in this world can beat the connection with another human being. And when that connection leads to love and loyalty, there's not much that can break it.

======= ◆ =======

———————— ◆ ————————

We all experience loss at some point in our lives. I am sure many of you already have, in some form or another. Don't live with regrets. Don't leave something unsaid, and most of all, never let something petty get in the way of family or friends. There are days when each step you take feels like the hardest, the most difficult—as if it will all crumble around you at any moment. During those days, never lose hope, or stop dreaming. Do your best to allow love into your heart—no matter what. Any direction in life, other than backward, is a success and should be celebrated.

———————— ◆ ————————

I love you, depending on who and how it's said, can hold so much meaning. No matter the intent, those three words represent a bond— they give strength—they let you know that no matter what may come your way, it's never gone through alone. Saying I Love You is simply one heart telling another, 'I will hurt with you, and I will hope with you.'

―――――――― ◈ ――――――――

We put great expectations on tomorrow when we truly need to rely on our current selves. Far too many overlook personal action as a means to get things done. Blame is easily passed if one does not hold themselves accountable. Own it— the good, the bad, the broken pieces, the uncontrollable happiness, the disappointment, and the smiles—own it all.

―――――――― ◈ ――――――――

———————— ◆ ————————

There always seems to be so much loss in the world, or maybe I'm just in tune with how precious life is, and I understand the finality of it all. Although our loved ones may have left this space in their physical form, they are always with us. Never doubt that. The connections we make are eternal.

———————— ◆ ————————

— ◆ —

Memories can flood the mind any time, carrying pieces of lost love or thoughts of loved ones. They can be beautiful and, at times, full of torment—what could have been—what was— what can never be again. Cherish the beautiful times, even if they are a bit jagged.

— ◆ —

As I've grown older, I believe we are set on a predestined path. The journey isn't always straight—there are twists, turns, and obstacles to overcome, but the journey's end remains. Our soul helps navigate the curves and gets us over the hurdles, bringing us closer to where we belong each day.

====== ◆ ======

Forever only lasts as long as we allow it or when some outside force beyond our control intervenes. Each day we must commit to living our best life and loving freely for as long as possible.

====== ◆ ======

———————— ◈ ————————

It seems more and more people feel the need to be unkind or indifferent, forgetting they're not the only ones hurting, suffering, or struggling at times. Remember, we're all going through a lot of the same things. They may not be the same, but we are all on similar paths. When you can, be empathetic. Be willing to understand the other side. Sometimes the simple act of listening can make all the difference—so many wish to conquer when all we truly need is to encourage.

———————— ◈ ————————

═══════ ◆ ═══════

The wars we wage on ourselves are like no other. Bad days may come but, on those days, when you may not feel your most vital, never admit defeat—you are not weak. It's during that time when things seem to be at their darkest, your inner strength will help to break down the barriers of doubt and keep the walls from closing in.

═══════ ◆ ═══════

———— ◆ ————

We all need that one person who will be there for us even during those moments we can't be there for ourselves.

———— ◆ ————

———— ◆ ————

There is a moment in all of our lives that forever changes us. For some, it may come early in the form of childhood tragedy. Others are fortunate enough to elude it far into adulthood. Whether it arrives through simply living life or enduring unimaginable loss, it's something we all experience. It may not be fully understood then, but it becomes like a retroactive epiphany, creating an imaginary divide between who we were and who we are. The two are entirely different, and there is no going back.

———— ◆ ————

=========== ◈ ===========

We all have a bit of darkness in our lives. Maybe a past that does not agree with us. One that we can't always get away from. But it's important not to live in that past, especially when you're alone. Do the best you can to not let those thoughts rule your world. Live in your light.

=========== ◈ ===========

―――――――― ◆ ――――――――

A day can feel like the shortest time ever. They seem to pass right into the next in a blink. Unless you're longing for someone, wishing for something, or wanting an outcome— a day can't end quickly enough.

―――――――― ◆ ――――――――

===== ◆ =====

So many feel as if they are less than a person because they've experienced bad situations in their lives. Everyone has been damaged and scarred in some capacity—no one is immune from terrible times. What's even worse is most times, they are the ones who dish out the hardest-hitting self-criticism. One cannot grow when thoughts are filled with negativity. There's enough pushing back against you in life. Don't be the cause of your own faded bloom.

===== ◆ =====

———————— ◈ ————————

We all have that 'one.' The one who got away. The one, all other things in life seem to be compared to. The one wilted rose between all of the thorns, pressed into a book of memories. The one who your mind runs to even when you can't. Certain people you just can't shift from your thoughts. And if they're taking up that much space, maybe they belong there.

———————— ◈ ————————

———— ◆ ————

You can't force something that isn't wanted or meant to be. Don't allow wishes to go wasted when a world of opportunities awaits you.

———— ◆ ————

———— ◈ ————

Starting over or second chances are privileges not everyone gets to experience. Imagine clearing the slate and stepping into the rest of your life with the knowledge you hold and none of the past disappointments. It's more feasible and attainable than one would think. Our self-doubt holds us back from so much, including doing what makes us happy and truly finding inner peace.

———— ◈ ————

I've always said every wrong turn taken has gotten me to the right place. That is so true in all of our lives. Whatever road we are on may be full of winding turns and curves, but the destination remains the same. It's the journey that changes. Navigate it best you can, even if the lines aren't drawn out for you. Light your own path.

━━━━━━━━ ◈ ━━━━━━━━

Sharing as much time with someone you love is priceless. Enjoy each moment you can, even if those moments may seem minor or insignificant. Remember none of them are ever guaranteed.

━━━━━━━━ ◈ ━━━━━━━━

Things usually end badly, or else they never end. Endings can sometimes be a blessing because they free you and open you up for new opportunities you may not have seen because of the stressed-out environment you remained in.

═══════════ ◆ ═══════════

How many of us try to keep ourselves busy, so the mind doesn't wander to thinking about things better left alone? Probably most of us. The past isn't always done with us, no matter how far we try to separate ourselves from it. Don't forget those times helped you grow and were steppingstones to where you are today. Use those lessons to light your future.

═══════════ ◆ ═══════════

—— ◆ ——

Is it fate? Destiny? Coincidence? I guess it could be all the above. It depends on who you ask. But I whole-heartedly believe certain people are supposed to cross your path at the right time and are with you no longer than is needed. Sometimes that's a season. Sometimes that's a lifetime.

—— ◆ ——

═══════ ◆ ═══════

No matter how far off course you go or how big the detour is, the finish line never changes. Keep your eyes forward because there's no way to get there looking backward.

═══════ ◆ ═══════

———————— ◆ ————————

If you find love in your heart, don't allow your mind to manifest a reason why it won't work. Let your heart do its job—love, without fear.

———————— ◆ ————————

===== ◈ =====

The most extraordinary love story you will ever know is the one shared with yourself. Be sure to treat yourself right because the relationship is the longest one you'll ever be a part of. We are what we accept, so expect the best. Love yourself completely, and you'll know what you deserve.

===== ◈ =====

———— ◆ ————

Life is lived and lost in the moments. Split seconds can make all the difference. Cherish all of them. Don't simply wait for the big finish, or you'll miss all the magic.

———— ◆ ————

━━━━━ ◆ ━━━━━

Do not disturb old feelings once they have found their final resting place. They are buried for a good reason: the lesson was learned, the damage was done, or it was time to move on. You can't allow yourself to be pulled down the same path once again. We look in the review mirror all too often. Most times, it's in the past because it belongs there. Life cannot be fully lived when the past is still part of your future. Let the memories that remain lie where you left them.

━━━━━ ◆ ━━━━━

―――――― ◆ ――――――

So many underestimate the real value of a kiss. From friendship to love, it holds true meaning. Sometimes a kiss says more than any words could ever. The kiss speaks in silence, expressing what words cannot.

―――――― ◆ ――――――

———— ◈ ————

Sometimes paths cross several times before they start running together. When those who are meant to find each other begin that journey as one, it's beautiful. At that moment, you know every wrong turn you have ever taken has gotten you to the right place.

———— ◈ ————

═══════════ ◆ ═══════════

The loss of a loved one is never easy. I believe they become an eternal light that shines in our lives, even after they're gone. And when I am unsure and find myself mystified by the trials of life, I look to the night sky with wonder and hope that I'm right.

═══════════ ◆ ═══════════

―――――――――― ◆ ――――――――――

Most live by the adage, 'strike while the iron is hot,' but I feel at times we do better when we share the warmth. We need compassion and mercy, not aggression and indifference, during the darkest days.

―――――――――― ◆ ――――――――――

———— ◈ ————

Be proud of your lineage. Your life was made possible because of the struggles and sacrifices made by others. There is no repayment; just continue to do your best to keep the name unsoiled.

———— ◈ ————

━━━━━━━ ◆ ━━━━━━━

As we get older, it's tough to find someone who hasn't been tainted by some relationship from their past. All we can do is be there for them and pick up any pieces that fall so they can remain whole.

━━━━━━━ ◆ ━━━━━━━

———— ◆ ————

The beauty of life and love is there's always a chance—an opportunity to improve on it or a time to overcome. There can be an open door to happiness that awaits even the most jagged of hearts. No matter the loss, love will forever find a way. The paths we've taken, and the people we have met, are all critical points along the journey. They are all pivotal moments spent serendipitously searching for the destination. Never think it's too late for opportunities, love, chasing a dream, or following your heart—it's not. Embrace every moment you have.

———— ◆ ————

========= ◆ =========

Don't live in fear of showing your true self. Life needs to be embraced, and as we evolve, we find who we are meant to be. Regrets should never be what fills our last thoughts.

========= ◆ =========

———— ◆ ————

There's nowhere to go when you find yourself in a one-way dead-end relationship. Don't invest any time in those who won't walk with you towards your goals. Love has to be a two-way street, or you'll find yourself wandering alone too far from home to find your way back.

———— ◆ ————

═══════════ ◆ ═══════════

Do not try to tame what was born free. A cage is no place to realize your dreams. Being chained in place is not considered living. Control yourself but never lose your ability to be absolutely spontaneous. Allow your wings to ride the wind and stay forever wild.

═══════════ ◆ ═══════════

———————— ◆ ————————

Mercy is divine intervention from the universe, and hope is the inner workings of positive outcomes. These two silent forces work in unison to help deliver us to the next stop along our journey.

———————— ◆ ————————

＝＝＝＝＝＝＝ ◈ ＝＝＝＝＝＝＝

Life is truly made from a series of ups and downs. It's never the big bang moments. It's those moments between the ohhhs and ahhhs that we'll never forget. It's those moments of unexpected bliss that make all the difference.

＝＝＝＝＝＝＝ ◈ ＝＝＝＝＝＝＝

—————————— ◆ ——————————

If you have a dream, never lose sight of it. Failure is a better motivator than success. Chasing dreams isn't ever easy, and it's the reason why so many settle for mediocre. Failing isn't an option for those who dare go after the golden ring. So when they fall, they get back up with a vengeance, and even more effort goes into getting to the goal.

—————————— ◆ ——————————

＝＝＝＝＝ ◈ ＝＝＝＝＝

Every moment in life teaches us a lesson. The
good ones go without saying, but the bad ones
teach us what we don't want, what we shouldn't
accept, and what can never happen again. Life
lessons are an endless learning tool—listen.

＝＝＝＝＝ ◈ ＝＝＝＝＝

Life is much better when you learn from living rather than worrying about being perfect. Don't wait for everything to be in place to start. Perfection is unattainable. There will always be something to tweak, change, or make better. Standing still keeps you from reaching your goal. Never restrain yourself with the weight of perfection. If you want to make a difference, if you intend to reach your goals, if you seek to attain your dreams—start today.

——— ◆ ———

You'll piss off many people when you start doing what's right for you. Those are the ones who would rather see you fail than succeed. Keep your head high. Never break yourself for someone else. By putting yourself last, you dull your shine, and that does no one any good.

——— ◆ ———

‒‒‒‒‒‒‒ ◈ ‒‒‒‒‒‒‒

Love is both complicated and straightforward. It's not tangible. It cannot be picked up, shared, bought, or stolen. Love is everything, and it is nothing. It is sleepless nights and days filled with bliss. If only those who seek it out understood love has no due date. Love can leave a scar if you become tangled in its relentless throws caused by desperation. For those with pure intentions, love will find you when it's least expected. It's important to remember that love also enters through closed doors.

‒‒‒‒‒‒‒ ◈ ‒‒‒‒‒‒‒

———— ◆ ————

Sometimes I reflect on the things life has given me and all that's been taken away, including those I've loved and lost—precious moments caught in time. Simple memories spread out before me—timeless reminders of how life goes on, even when it feels like you cannot.

———— ◆ ————

======== ◆ ========

I want to live my life truly happy. To wake up each morning and face the day with a smile, as if I am living out a daydream. Hard work and sacrifices should be rewarded with a willing heart to share the beating, a gentle touch to soothe the soul, and a soft place to land when the world spins out of control.

======== ◆ ========

There's a moment just after the day breaks which offers an early glimpse of what's to come. In those precious instances, we can elect to embrace all that stands before us or pull and push against it. Each and every day we are given a fresh chance, a blank page to write into history. Choose your memories wisely, because after it's all said and done, they are all we have.

So often, many lose sight of the desire to accomplish anything for themselves. Instead, most seek acceptance, being noticed, or proving someone wrong. There's far too much value put on the opinion of others over our own. We build a wall out of the perceptions of others, and then we struggle to find ourselves within those visions. All that does is leaves us fighting for our own acceptance and continue to allow them to create the box for which we remain. How we see ourselves sets the blueprint for how everyone else treats us. Treat yourself kind, or no one else will.

---◆---

As kids, we have no real inhibitions. As we grow older, we stop enjoying things the way we once did. We're taught fear, the 'right way to do things,' and humility. I used to love running through puddles after a good rainstorm, no matter the size. My clothes couldn't soak through fast enough. I still have memories of my grandmother mad as hell because I would walk barefoot everywhere I went during my summers in Florida. There wasn't a challenge I couldn't defeat. Youth isn't wasted on the young, we just allow it to grow old. Somewhere along the line, I stopped coming home drenched. I stopped needing to wash my feet before I walked through the door. I want that all back. I want to live and love fearlessly. I want to stand in the middle of a thunderstorm, my head pointed towards the sky, with a smile and a wink as if to say, "Let's get wet!"

---◆---

---◆---

We exist in extremely troubling times. Even though the wolf at the door seems relentless, never lose the will to survive. Living with a pure heart gives the soul strength to outlast the wickedness.

---◆---

———————— ◆ ————————

When you don't feel worthy of it, love will always find a way. While you're walking through hell, you will find heaven. It will keep you safe from harm, carry you high and get you home.

———————— ◆ ————————

———— ◈ ————

Little by little, we come to realize that as much as we try and mold ourselves into who we want to be, our surroundings and situations win out more times than not. Sometimes in life, we hit hurdles and instead of jumping over them, to stay on our path, we allow them to control the next move. Those choices all come with consequences, both good and bad. There are times when we block our own well-being, simply because we don't feel worthy. The walls of self-doubt can take years to break down. Know that you are worth it and deserving of happiness and more importantly, love. Don't ever lose your joy. Take comfort in the choices you have made; each one has been vital in helping you face the life ahead of you.

———— ◈ ————

Most times, the journey is often more important than the destination. Life is about enjoying the ride. It is important to remain unpretentious. Your day doesn't have to be a mad dash to tomorrow. Always take strides to keep going forward but stay focused on what's important. There will be days when you are flying high and others when you can't seem to get your feet off the ground. Enjoy every moment—even those that aren't pleasant—each one will leave a lesson.

=========== ◆ ===========

The happiest of hearts don't always carry the most joy. All too often those who have been shattered before, continue to pump love out to those around them. And although the pieces are never put back together quite the same, the light still shines. Never live without purpose. Rage like a roaring fire, with the control and power of a lover's whisper.

=========== ◆ ===========

========= ◈ =========

Life is short and we are dead a long time. Never get so used to something that we forget how important the little things in life are. Take time to truly live, not simply go through life. Give trust to everyone, until they show reason not to. Don't be fooled by lust or force yourself to love – it should come naturally. And most of all – let the people in your life who mean the most – know they do - EVERY CHANCE YOU CAN because one day you won't have that opportunity.

========= ◈ =========

=========== ◆ ===========

As a storyteller, I can create vast worlds with whoever and whatever I choose. Reality isn't that easy, and it's probably best left that way. Life is meant to be lived, which means experiencing it, not relying on fantasy.

=========== ◆ ===========

Final Word ━━━━━

It wasn't until after my father was gone, that I was able to look back on things and understand what a strong and brilliant man he truly was - humble, goodhearted, compassionate to a point, and he took absolutely no bullshit. He wanted me to learn for myself what repercussions came from the decisions I made. He wanted me to experience life, first-hand, not from some path he or anyone else carved out for me. I have come to realize life is beautiful and at times simple, but never easy. Because of that, I was able to learn the ways of the world long before I'd have to put the knowledge to use.

I often wonder if I've broken the vessel. Is the hardened shell already cracked? Has exposing the soul inside to the ways of this world tainted my inner peace, or has it simply allowed me to grow an understanding that we all face this world alone but surrounded by countless warriors fighting the same daily battle.

Celebrate victories but remember each of those battles. Life will leave scars but each one represents survival. As we get older and gain experience, it's important to realize each stone along the journey is a step closer in our search for a higher meaning.

I want to leave you with one last wish. My wish for you is during your most ominous days, the shadows will hold you close and never let you go. I hope you find a sparkle in each new breath and know the world would be a much darker place without your light. Find passion within the slightest of shines and remember roots will grow wherever you are.

Jay Long

Jay on Jay ══════

I am a New York based writer and poet. I grew up in the awe-inspiring Hudson Valley area, 60 miles from the greatest city in the world and smack dab in the middle of tranquility and grace. I have had a passion for writing since I was a small child. Being near the Hudson River and water has always helped me find my voice. I find clarity there and a simple no cost way to re-align when things get a bit askew.

Since I can remember, I have loved to write and tell stories. There has always been something special about pen and paper. As a child I remember sitting next to my mother with a yellow legal pad and black felt pen mimicking her cursive writing. Even today I prefer writing by hand to electronic means. I keep a spiral notebook in each room for anytime an idea may arise.

My love for words started when I discovered music. As a teenager anytime I'd get a new album, I'd immediately open up the lyric sheet to read the words even before I listened to the song. As you read in the introduction, my love of poetry began after reading Robert Frost's 'The Road Not Taken' in my college English class. It truly changed my life, as I felt I had always carved my own path, even at a young age.

At age 23 I wrote my first screenplay. While I had no real knowledge of how to market my work, and living on the east coast, I tried a few query letters and continued to write. That same year I started writing my second screenplay, but as life and responsibility took over, I put my writing to the back burner and changed my priorities until recently. In December of 2013, I created a Facebook page to share my writing. Since that time, the Writer Jay Long page has attracted over 150K followers.

Storytelling, and expressing feelings through words are what I am best at. There is nothing like having someone use my words to help heal. Writing allows for the 'perfect' ending to any situation.

I enjoy connecting with fans and sharing pieces of myself with the world. I am following my dreams and traveling down a path that was laid out many years ago. I love hearing how others connect and can relate to my writing.

I hope you enjoyed this collection of thoughts. If you did, I would greatly appreciate you leaving a review on your favorite platform for books.

If you'd like to share a cup of coffee with me, you can do that as well. buymeacoffee.com/jaylong

Thank you.

Jay Long

Facebook.com/writerjaylong

Instagram.com/writerjaylong